Scribbles & Notes

A Collection of Reflections

N. Barber

Made with ❤ on the BookLeaf Publishing Platform
www.bookleafpub.in
www.bookleafpub.com

Dedication

To my Lord & Savior, Jesus Christ,
To my Pops, &
To the love of my life, Hannah

I don't know where I'd be in this life without any of these rocks in my life.

Preface

I don't truly know where to begin with this book. I am no poet, I am no scholar, I AM just a guy who loves the Lord and loves to love people. I hope the words of this book will touch the heart and soothe the mind. I will do my best to fumble through each of these daily musings to come up with something of quality. I have always enjoyed the exploration of putting words to paper from a young age and have always found poetry to be such an interesting place to reflect on everything. These are simply reflections from moments of emotion, worship, love, and overwhelming gratitude. Thank you for your time.

Acknowledgements

There are so many people I could acknowledge who have been in my life and been such a connection that I need to mention... I could honestly fill this book with those names, but I will at least say this:

To my dearest friends, to my mentors along the way, to each one whom I've shared a meaningful moment with you,

You are **_worthy_**, you are **_enough_**, and

you are loved.

1. What A Friend

What a friend we have in thee
The blameless lamb upon a tree
A broken man in the tomb
The sacrifice for all rage and ruin

What a friend we have in thee
Spilt his blood for you, for me
The only Son come down from above
To save the souls for all in His love

What a friend we have in thee
Third Days Dawn is rising, as is He
The stone has rolled and He awoke
Death was defeated as He spoke

What a friend we have in thee
The sacrifice for all to see
The light of life shining through
Behold Him now, the way, life, and truth

What a friend we have in thee
A blameless lamb upon the tree
Our broken savior in the tomb
Our sacrifice for all rage and ruin

What a friend we have in thee
My Jesus, Savior, and Risen King

2. The Three

The three along the road, I'm laying in the ditch
Broken, beaten, bruised, without a hope
The first looks upon me, turns his head away
The second? Well, the second does the same
The third, a man against me, **or so that's what I think**
The third, He reaches out, and He pulls me to my feet
He healed me, fixed me, provided for me
You, Lord, You did the same

3. But Christ the Last

Satan had the first word, **but Christ the last.**
You shattered the mirror that reflects my past
The brokenness of my sinful soul was washed white
In the devastating beauty of the heavenly blood's flow

How great thou art, how deep thine love
How sweet your grace that ever comes
To save the sinners, to redeem the lost
To bring us all from the deepest loss

Eternal separation is the enemies goal
To pull us from the Father's hold
The lake of fire to be our forever home
The earthly flesh and desires there within
Toils and snares released to sin
My brokenness, the darkest pit
I lay in death, Filling emptiness with emptiness

But God.

Sent his everlasting, his only
The blameless, friend of sinners
The spotless, Son of Man
The sacrificial, Holy of Holys
The King of Kings, Yeshua
Jesus.
Bridged the gap, tore the veil
Paid the price

May we never lose hope, lose sight,
Nor may we lose the light but bask in His.
Take heart, sinner.

Satan had the first word, but Christ the last.

4. Behold

In the waiting, in the suffering
In the crushing and the breaking
In the healing, in the fixing
In the growing pains of the seasons

I will behold you for who you are
I will behold you where er' I trod
I will behold you, your holy fire
I will behold you, my God

In the ashes of my smoldering soul
You're the spark that is the fuel
When life is a weight I cannot bear
When the answers seems to all but stop
And it feels like you're not there

I will behold you for who you are
I will behold you where er' I trod
I will behold you, your holy fire
I will behold you, my God

5. All Creation Sings

All creation sings
The birds, the bees, the rock & trees
Even the rocks cry out in song

All creation sings
The heavenly chorus belts out for the glory they see
Holy, holy, holy they cry out all the day long

All creation sings
My heart overflows from within
Dwelling in my soul is the one whom fills

All creation sings
The wind and waves
Worship whispers all throughout

All. Creation. Sings.

6. My God, My God

"My God, my God, why hast thou forsaken me?" the
man upon the tree cried,
"My God, my God, why is this the cup I bear, the burden
that I share for which I shall die?"

It would be so easy to see
All the reason you and me
Would've never made to this moment

The meek, the mild, the powerful, the wild
The Holy Lamb
The strong, the brave, the one who defeated the grave
Yeshua, Jesus Christ

The cost was counted
The debt paid
The grave was silent
Until the third day

My God, my God, why hast thou paid for me?

My God, my God, thank you for the man upon the tree.

The meek, the mild, the powerful, the wild
The Holy Lamb
The strong, the brave, the one who defeated the grave
Yeshua, Jesus Christ

My God, my God, why hast thou paid for me?
My God, my God, thank you for the man upon the tree.

7. Me?

Dad, Father, Papa, Abba
That position has always been a hard one
To see one whom is perfect willing to call me son

Me?
In my brokenness?
In my sin?
In my shame?

At my pit, **you picked me up**
At my broken, **you put me back together**
At my worse, **you made me better**

Abba, God, my Father
You saw me, you still see me
You held me, you still hold me
You've never forsaken me

You've never failed me

8. "Boy, Buck Up"

In the old hayfield
In the scratchy barn straw
Fond, fond memories lie
Memories of a time before it all went wrong

A simpler time when I hurt, I'd cry
I'd let emotions flow
Not afraid to show
The bottle open and overflowed

But the calluses grew,
"Boy buck up" was my taught truth
Push past the rejection and pain
Push past and mask it away

Where do I put it all when the well is run dry?
Where do I put it all when the bottles overflowed?
Where do I put it all in my fight or flight?
Where do I go?
Anywhere but here.

In the old hayfield
In the scratchy barn straw
I'm finding that time again
Back at the root of it all

9. Personal Ghost

Love is a beauty, a beautiful thing
Wrapped in enigma, signed by a ring
You are a treasure, a precious thing
I try to express but my words fail me

Marriage is a gift, your love? *The bow.*
If joy is wine, *my cup overflows*
And I'm still trying to wrap my head around
Your loves' affect, **so profound**

And if I were the first to go before you
I'd come back but not to haunt
Give you winks, signs, pokes, and prods
Whispers in the wind to let you know
That not even death could stop the tie between our souls
Oh, I won't let go

If I were the first, I'd come back to be your personal
ghost

10. Til'

Til' the day I die
Til' my last breath
Til' they lay me down for my eternal rest
Til' I'm done for, down the count
Til' the lights go out, the lights go out
You've got my love

Til' the bridges break
Til' the creeks rise
Til' the Lord no longer wills and I close my eyes
Til' I'm knocked out and they ring the bell
You've got my love

Til' that fateful day that I don't wake
Til' my dirt nap
Til' I can no longer wade this life's crap
Even after I reach eternity's shore
You've got my love

11. Casket Bed

Someone asked me once do I love you to death
I said whisper her name in my casket bed
And see the life inside me rise again
Like the morning sun in the valley

11. No Push, No Shove

A barren path, a beaten road
A mountain high, a valley low
Nowhere to hide, nowhere to go
Nothing to do, but turn to your call

Into your arms, into your love
Filled with your grace from up above
No worldly thing, no push, no shove
Could ever pluck me from your love

This rock I've found, tied to my leg
This chasm deep inside my head
This soul that yearns to be free
This heart that knows what must be done

Run to your arms, into your love
Filled with your grace from up above
No worldly thing, no push, no shove
Could ever pluck me from your love

All I am is all you need
What I can be is what you see
You call me out to draw me in
To take me away from the death of sin

Into your arms, into your love
Filled with your grace from up above
No worldly thing, no push, no shove
Could ever pluck me from your love

13. Blind

In the street, I'm Bartimaeus calling out to you
You know, though ask me what do I need?
My whole life *I've been blind please help me see*

Help me see the life inside your light
Help me see the joy, the strength, the peace
You're the way, the truth, the life
The death of death, the king of kings
I've been blind, help me see

14. I'm Trying

I'm trying to learn the practice of your presence
To meditate in the stillness, the quiet place where you
reside
I'm trying to find the moments where my heart and
mind
will just hush for a second to to rest in the wings of your
might
But I'm having such a hard time trying to find those
moments in my life

But you're not a whisper in the wind,
You're a roaring, raging fire
You're not just in the still and quiet,
You're in the busy and loud
You're with me everywhere,
Your presence surrounding
like an army, a cavalry
You're always on my side

I'm trying to sit in the moments when I don't feel it
To still understand that you're still there even then
I'm trying to follow even after I stumble
To know you're not just scolding me and given up

But you're not just a judge or angry father
You're a loving, merciful, graceful Abba
You're not just in the perfect times
You step into the mess of my life
You're with me every moment
Your presence surrounding
like a sweet, gentle father
You're always on my side

15. Wanderin', Ponderin', Searchin'

Wanderin'
Ramblin'
Searchin'

Wonderin'
Ponderin'
Thinkin'

Where do I go?
What do I do?
Who even am I anymore?

Never thought I'd make it
Thought I was lost and forever alone
Til' you came in
With the bright light you shone

No longer *wanderin'*
No longer *searchin'*

Because in You,
I found home

16. Digging

Emptiness filling emptiness
A hole ran deep
Always searching endlessly
For the piece to feel complete

Hoping, wishing, waiting
Digging further and further
The dirt and sweat of shame spatter my face
My search for some type of "treasure" continues with
such fervor

I never realized I'd never find it there
My eyes were turned inward
No chance of me to find you
My identity lost, broken, splintered

One day, at the bottom of my self-dug pit
I turned my head upward in desperation
To see You waiting with a rope tossed down
You pulled me up, placed me on the firm foundation

Lost, broken, gone
Was all that I was
Found, complete, home
To bring people there, is now my cause

17. Ingrained

Til' death do us part
Doesn't equate when our hearts
And souls intertwined so deeply

Ingrained in one another
Two becoming one
One becoming *whole*

Til' death do us part
Doesn't apply as death is just the start
Of a sweet, sweet eternity together

18. Love's Song

Love, sweet love
An enigma wrapped in bliss
Hate, dark hate
A power that never seems to quit

Anger, twisted anger
A place where hurt resides
Love, sweet love
The power to heal all mankind

While I'm no stranger to
The hate and the anger
My heart and my soul
Try to let love's song ring out like thunder

Won't you see? Won't you see?
If you could do the same
Respond with love, sweet love
Let that be what your heart proclaims

19. Such A Strange Thing

Loss & grief are such a strange thing
Can sweep into you, take your summer and spring
Turn your heart into cold, hard winter
Make you chilled to the bone, make you shake and
shiver

Loss & grief can strangely be a gift
Can patch together, the tides, the rifts
Piece by piece, the pain can be the glue
Make your heart fly to the heights it once flew

Loss & grief are such a strange thing
Loss & grief are such a strange thing

20. Thank You, Thank You

Thank you, thank you
To those whom have shown love
To those whom have shown grace
To those whom have shown friendship

Thank you, thank you
To the ones who stuck with me
In the moments where I was not worth it
When I was self-centered and lost

Thank you, thank you
To the One who saved me
Picked me up in the pits of my despair
Brushed me off and showed me deepest love and care

Thank you, thank you
To my life's love
The partner sent after so many prayers to the One above
And shown me a love like
I've never seen here on Earth

Thank you, thank you
To the one's who left me
Helped me realize who I am
What I was hiding from in the facade of our friendships

Thank you, thank you
To anyone who's 'seen' me
To anyone who's taken the time to 'know' me
To anyone who's loved or been loved by me
Those moments are some of life's greatest gifts

Thank you, thank you.

21. Whom shall go?

Whom shall Go?
Here I am, send me
Send me to the hurt
Send me to the broken

May I be the hands and feet
To reach those with burdened souls
With hearts crumbled from defeat
Here I am, send me

May I be the ears and eyes
To listen to those who are battered and bruised
With bodies broken from the world's abuse
Here I am, send me

May I be the love and light
To brighten the darkness of
those who feel forgotten and lost
With souls like the darkness before dawn
Here I am, send me

Whom shall go?
Here I am, send me
Send me to the hurt
Send me to the broken

Whom shall go?
Here I am, send me

* 9 7 8 9 3 6 3 3 0 4 4 7 5 *